Seaforth Ontario in Colour Photos, Saving Our History One Photo at a Time

Photography
by Barbara Raué
2014

Series Name:
Cruising Ontario

Book 63: Seaforth

Cover photo: Seaforth Post Office

Series Name: Cruising Ontario
Saving Our History One Photo at a Time

Other Books by Barbara Raue

Coins of Gold

Arrows, Indians and Love

The Life and Times of Barbara
Volume 1: Inventions That Have Enhanced My Life
Volume 2: Entertainment That I Have Enjoyed
Volume 3: East Coast Trips
Volume 4: Olympics Have Always Intrigued Me
Volume 5: Wonders of the World
Volume 6: Caribbean Cruises We Have Enjoyed
Volume 7: Animals
Volume 8: Storms and Other Major Disasters in My Lifetime
Volume 9: Wars, Terrorist Attacks and Major Disasters

The Cromwell Family Book

Seaforth

Seaforth is a southern Ontario community in Huron County.

Originally known as *Four Corners* and *Steene's Corners* after an early settler, much of the area of what is now Seaforth was acquired by brothers Christopher and George Sparling in anticipation of the construction of the Buffalo, Brantford and Goderich Railway. Developer James Patton of Barrie purchased the land and laid out a town site in 1855.

Seaforth's Main Street is a Provincially Designated Heritage Conservation District, and architectural critics consider it to be one of the finest late 19th century streetscapes remaining in the Province.

A post office was established in Seaforth in 1859. In September 1876, at two o'clock in the morning, a fire broke out in Mrs. Griffith's Candy and Grocery store raging through Main Street destroying 12 acres of the business section. The town rebounded and Main Street was rebuilt with the brick and block structures which we see today, more than a century later. This architectural composition of two storey brick buildings is unique in its uniformity of scale and character. Through grants and local support, property owners have been encouraged to restore and preserve the architectural characteristics of their buildings so that this valuable resource may continue to be a reminder of Seaforth's history. The street is lined with uniquely homogeneous buildings and you will always know the time from one of the most lavish clocks of its day.

In 2001, Seaforth was amalgamated with Brussels, Grey Township, McKillop Township and Tuckersmith Township to form the Municipality of Huron East.

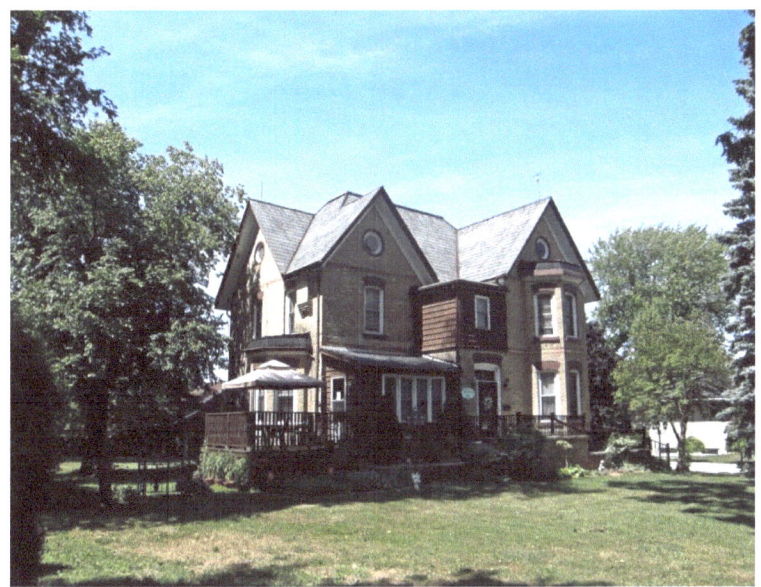

#143 – Queen Anne style

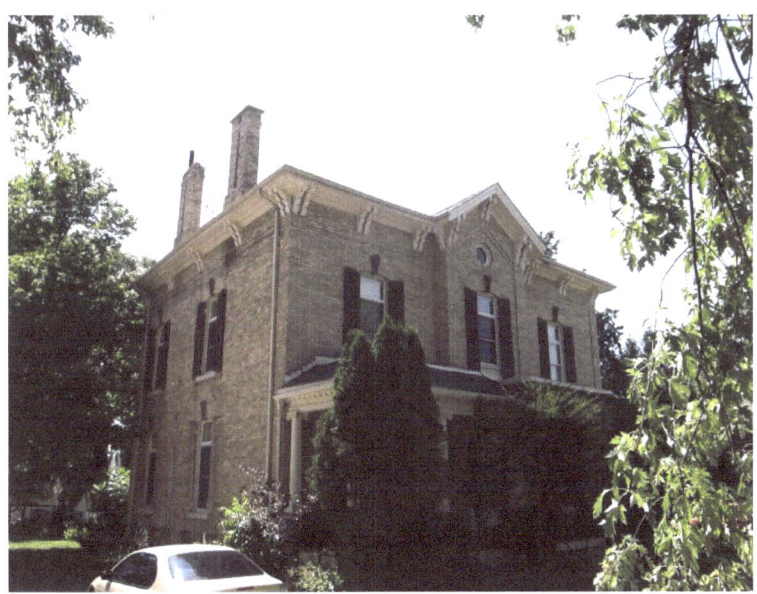

Italianate – cornice brackets

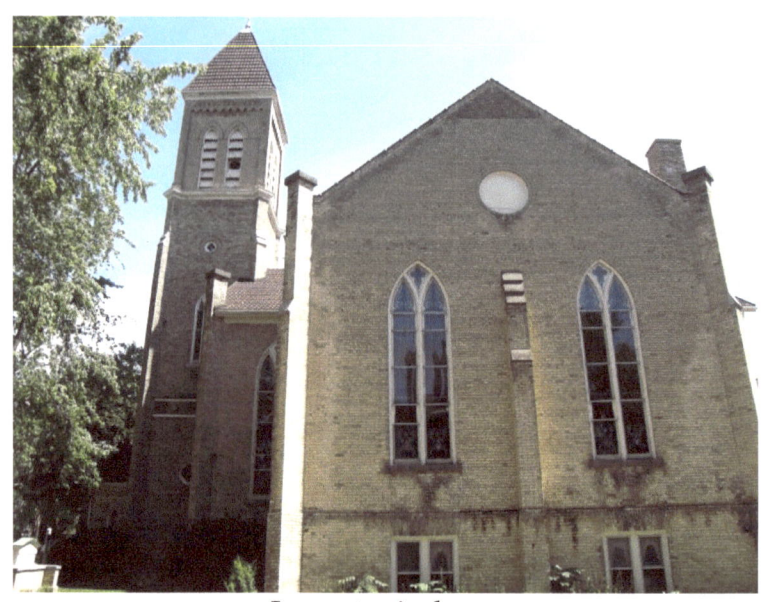

Lancet windows
#59 – First Presbyterian Church established 1867

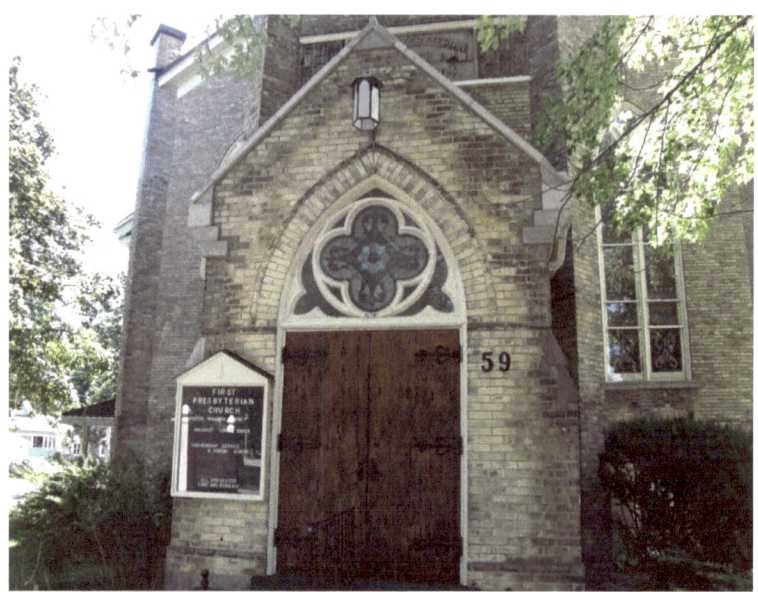

Rose window

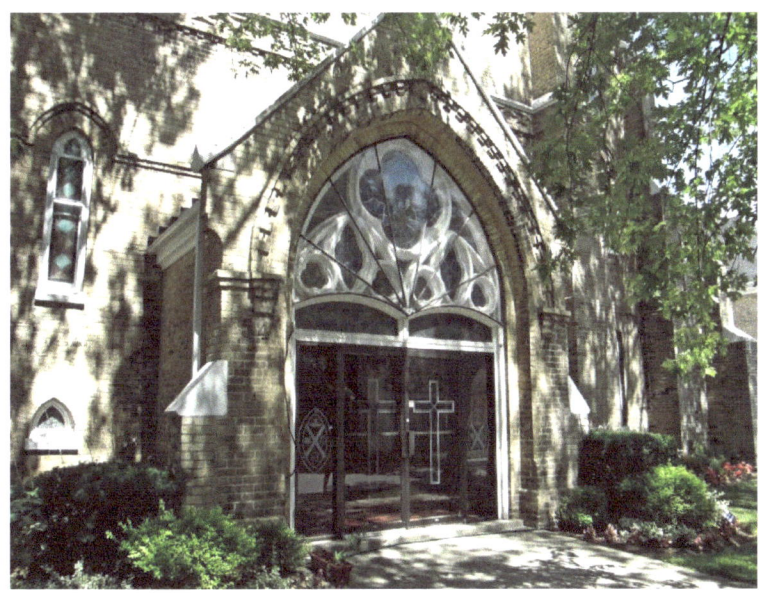

#54 – Methodist Church erected A.D. 1877

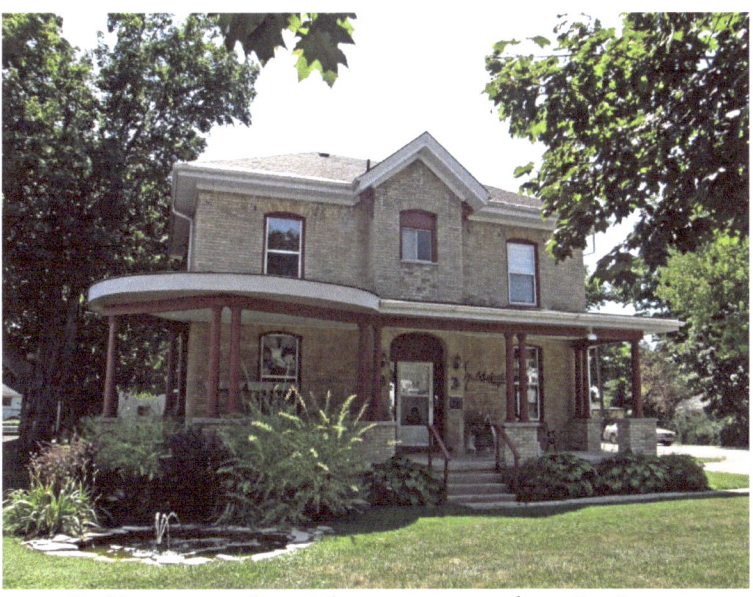

Italianate style with two-storey frontispiece,
wrap-around verandah

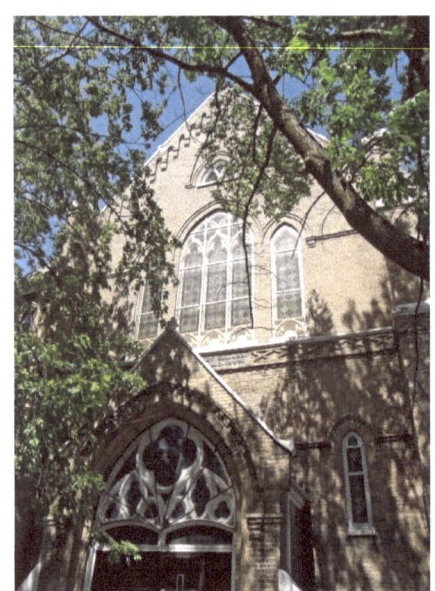
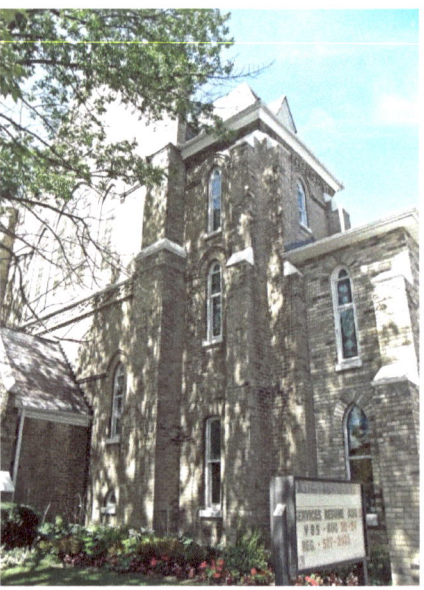

Northside United Church

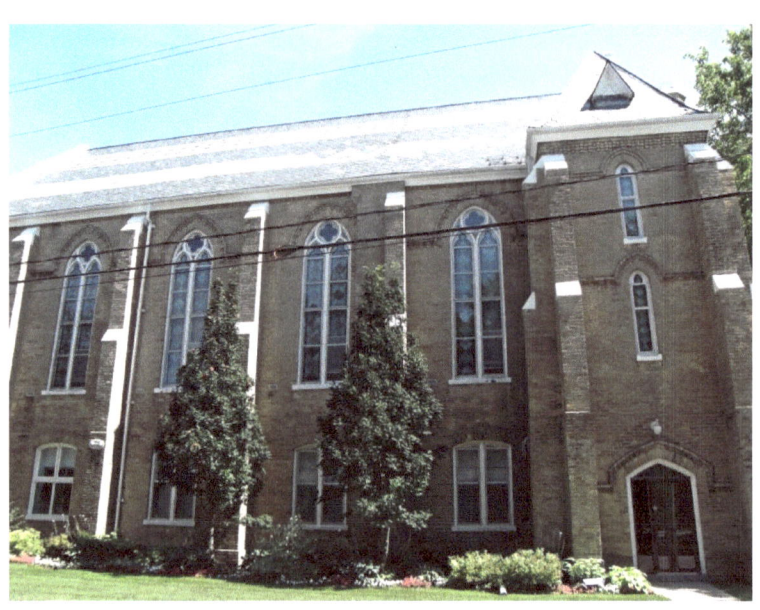

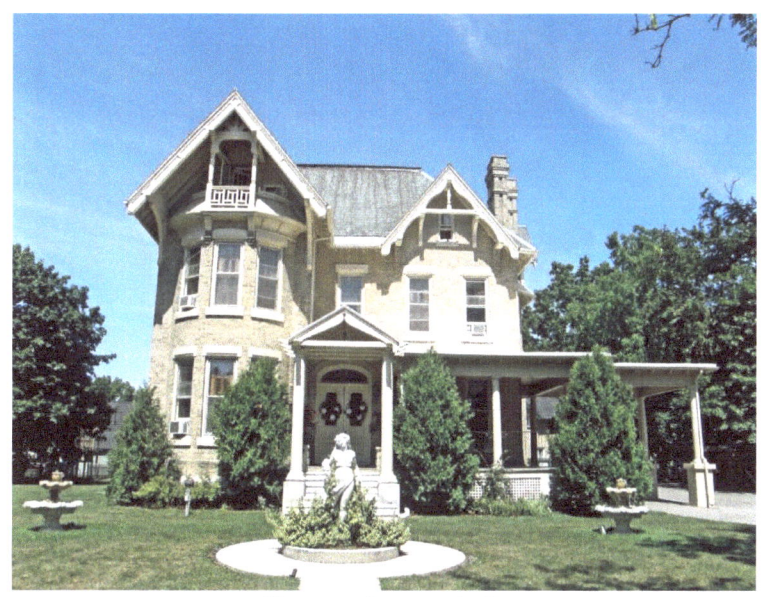

Queen Anne style

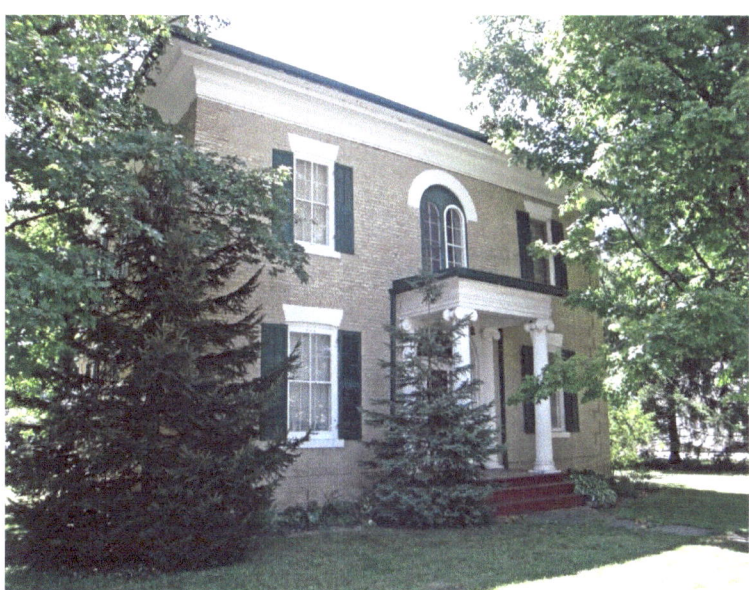

92 Goderich Street West – The Mullen House – Lorne Villa

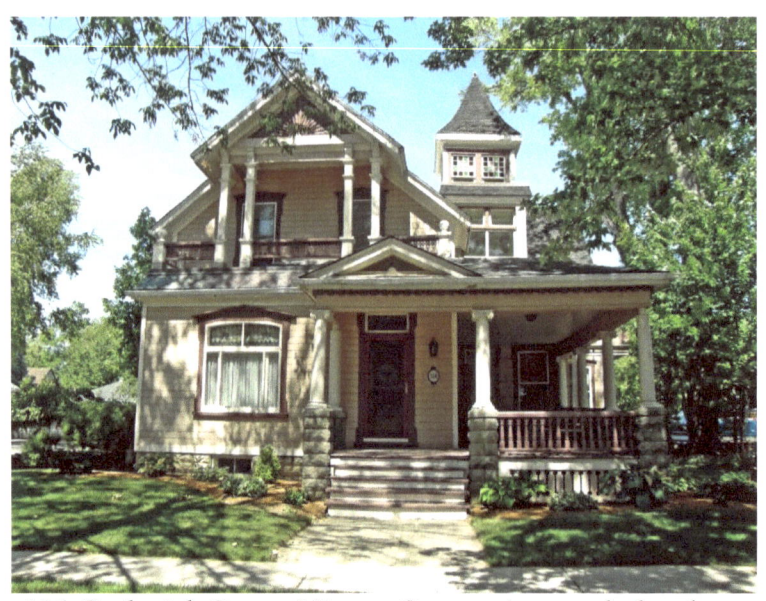

116 Goderich Street West – Queen Anne – belvedere, side verandah

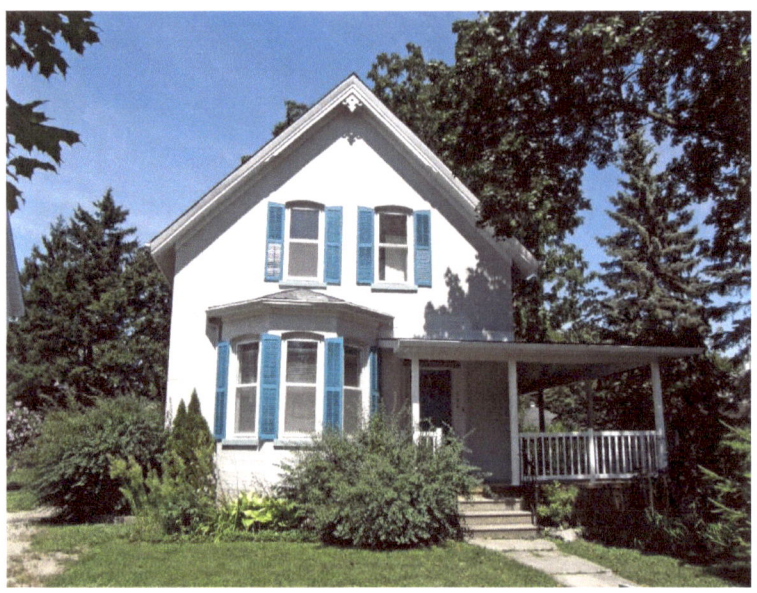

124 Goderich Street West - Gothic Revival

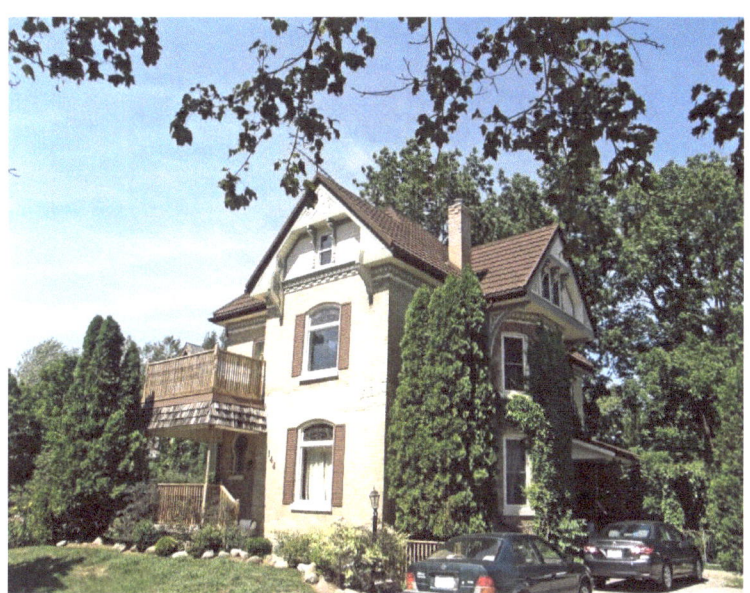

144 Goderich Street West – Gothic Revival

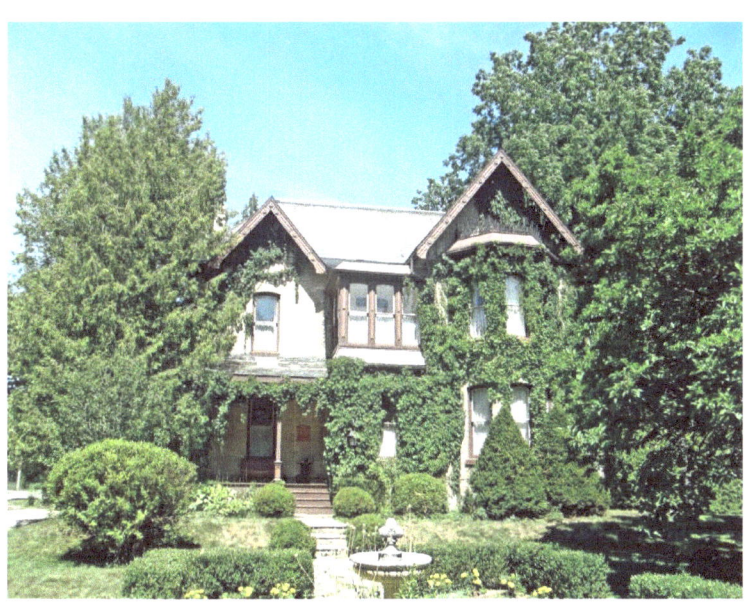

McLean House 1889 – Gothic Revival
- Carolin Shepherd M.D., Robert Shepherd PhD.

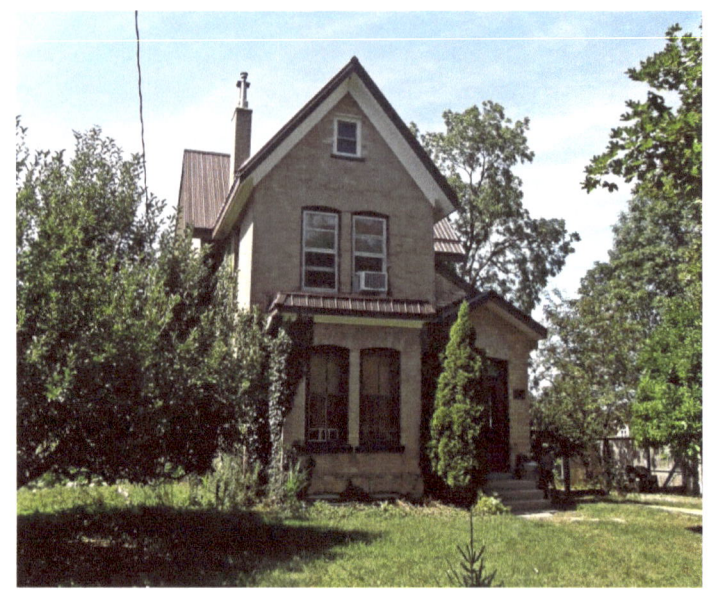

#19 – Gothic Revival

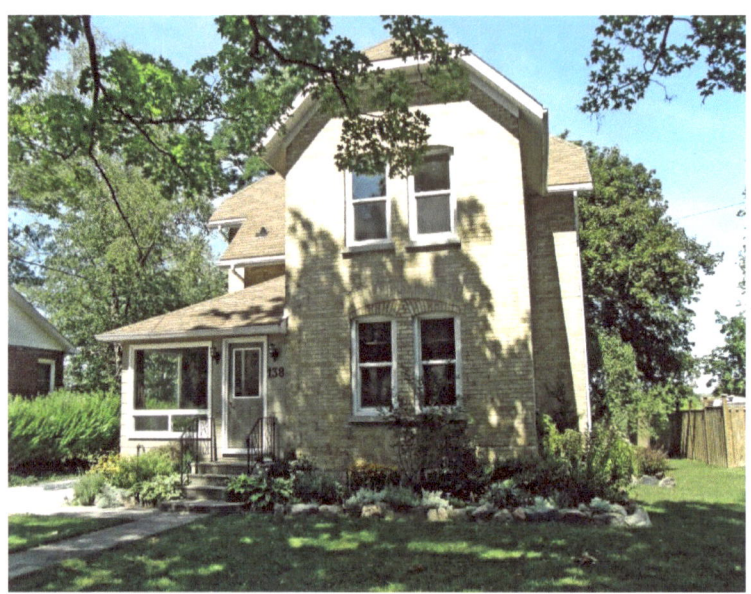

#138

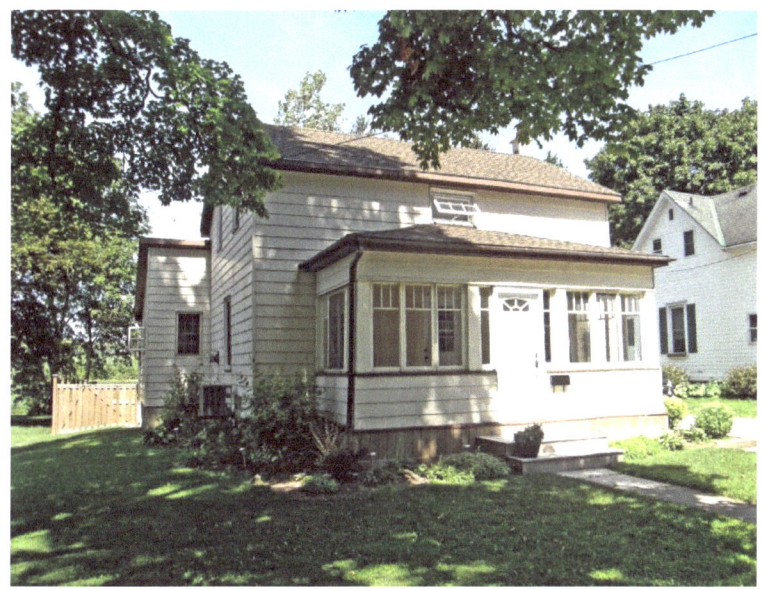

Gothic Revival – side gable

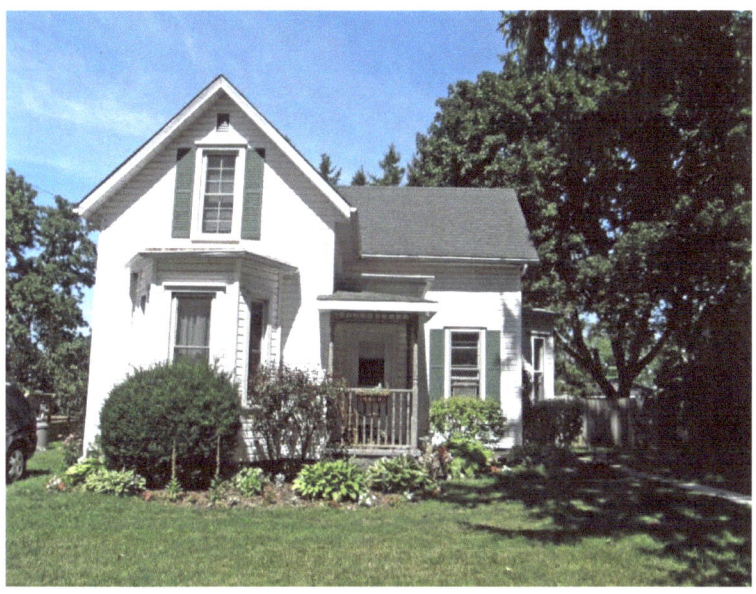

Gothic Revival

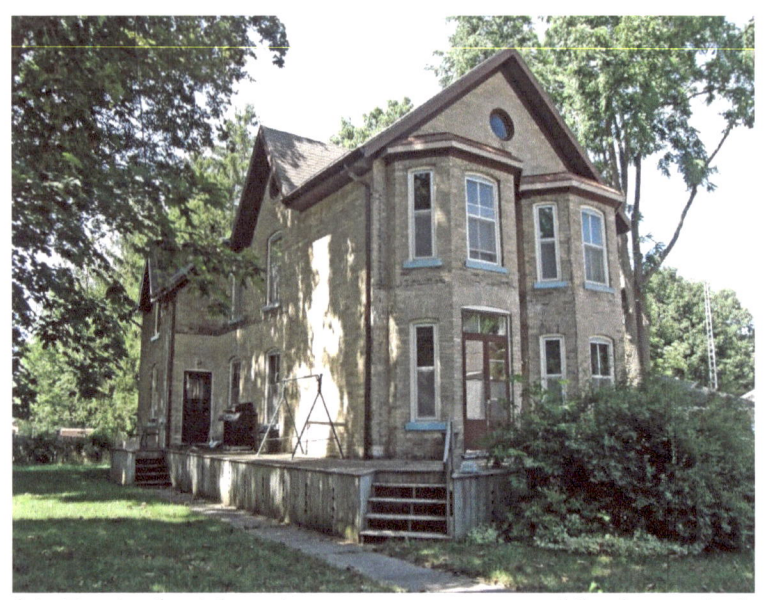

Gothic Revival with twin two-storey tower-like bay windows

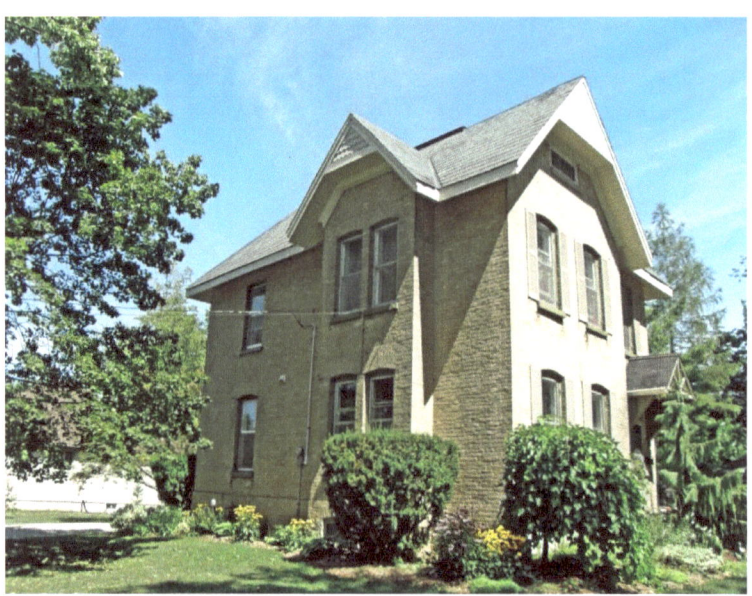

Gothic Revival

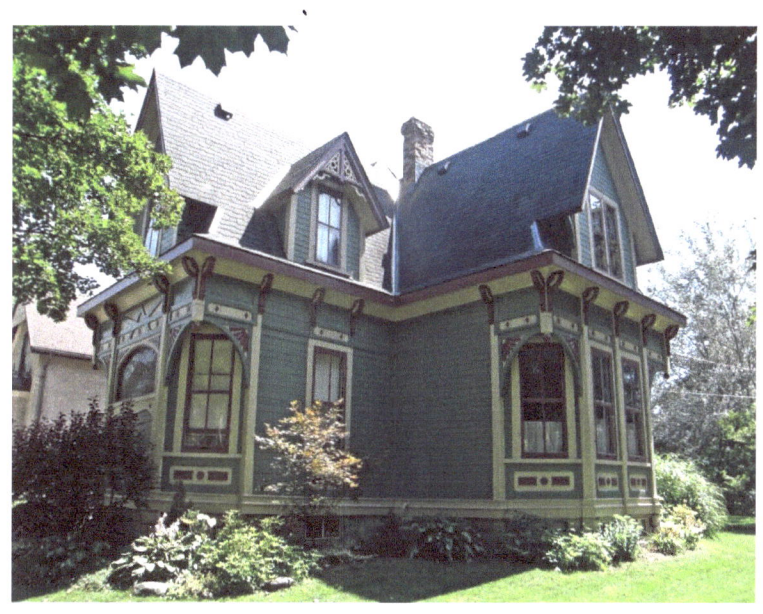

Queen Anne – decorative cornice brackets

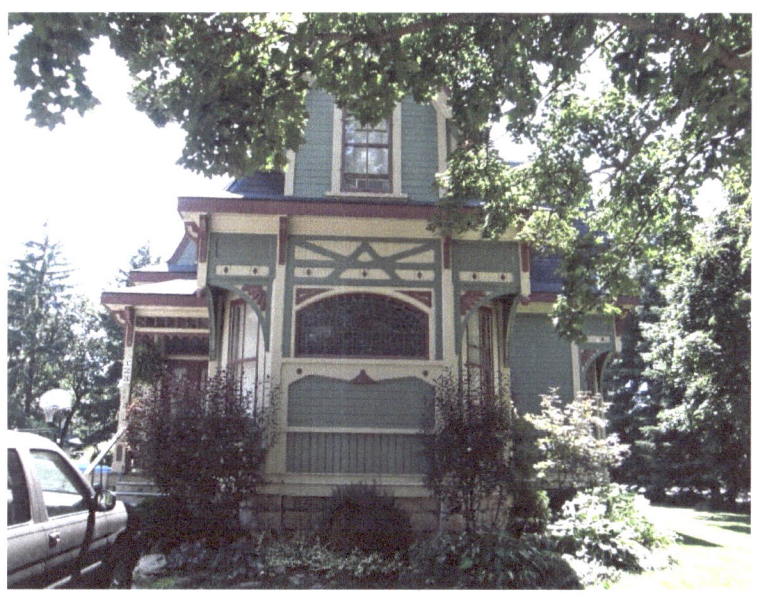

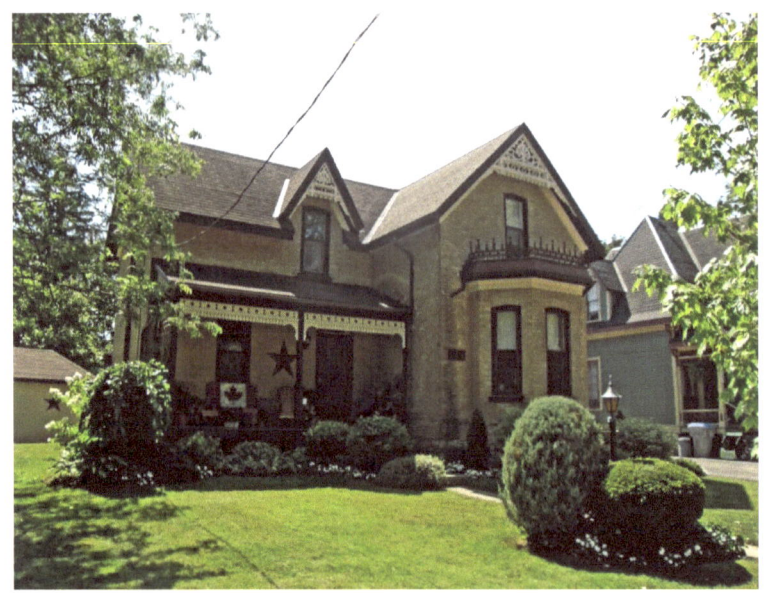

#119 - Gothic Revival – iron cresting above bay window

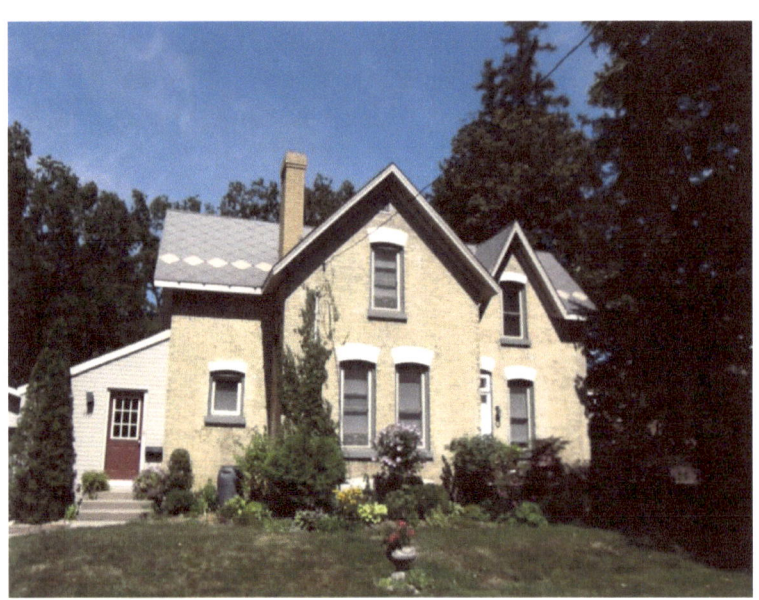

Gothic Revival – dichromatic roofing

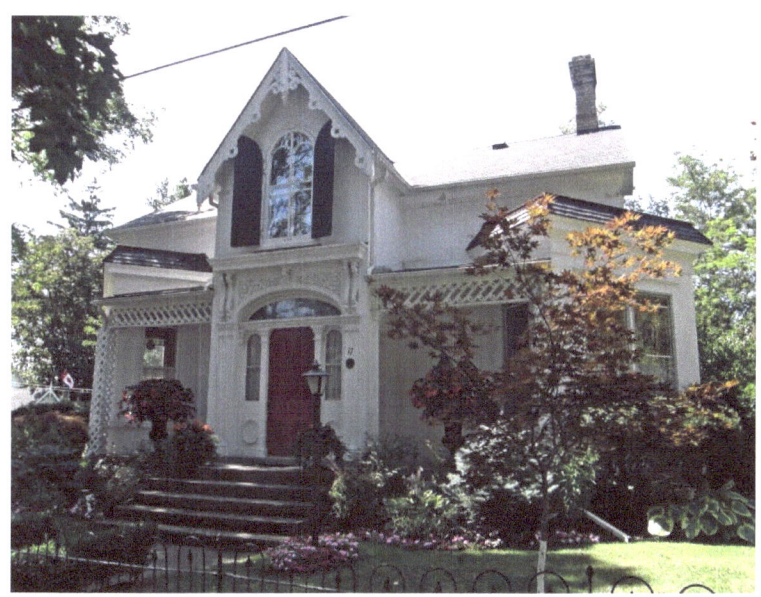

#17 – Gothic Revival – vergeboard trim on gable

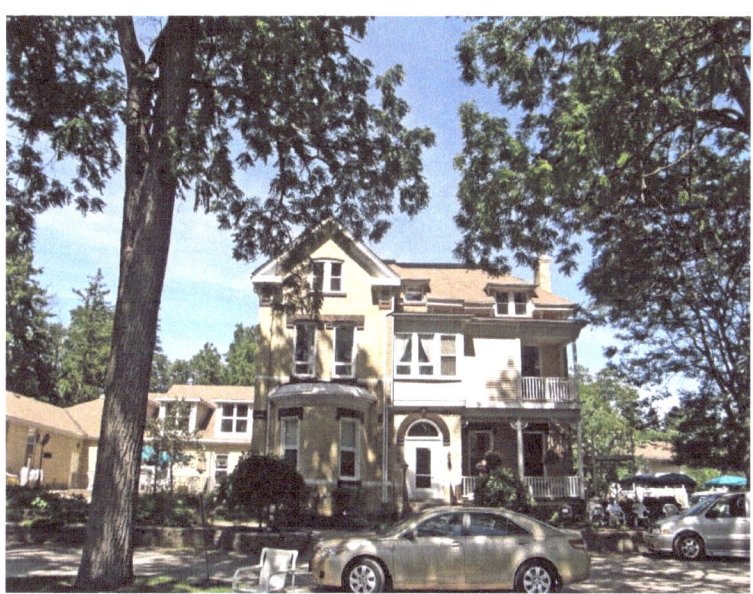

Seaforth Manor – Helen Street – cornice return on gable

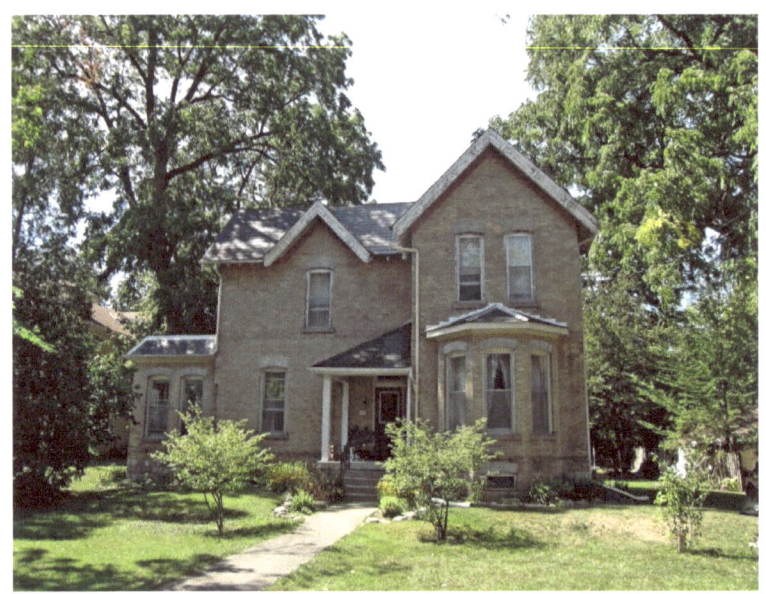

43 Helen Street – Gothic Revival

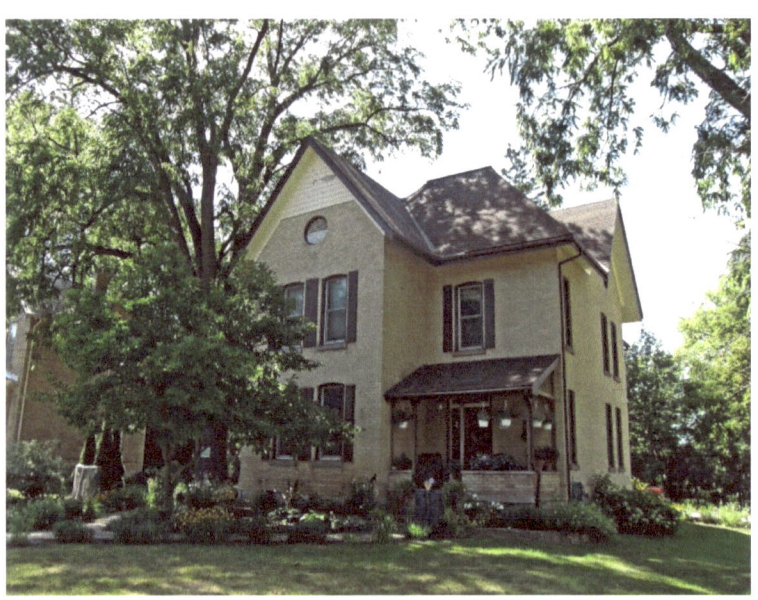

Gothic Revival

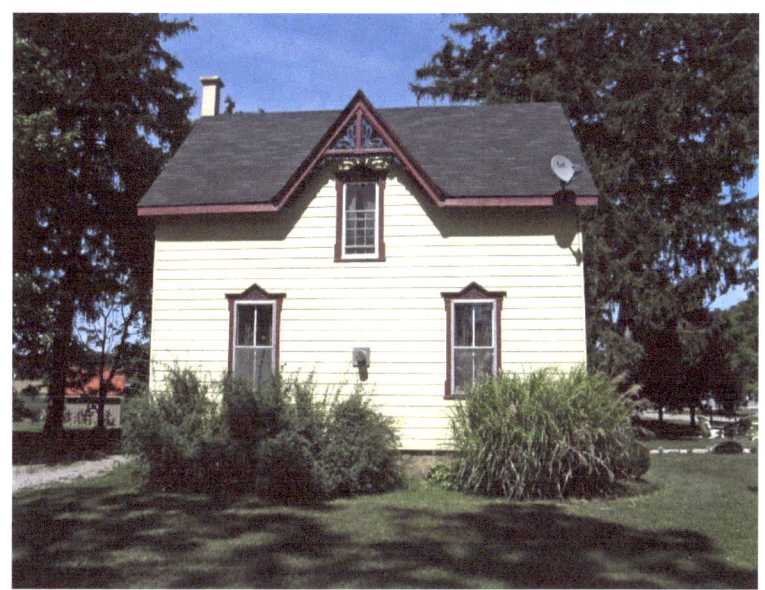

Gothic Revival, vergeboard trim

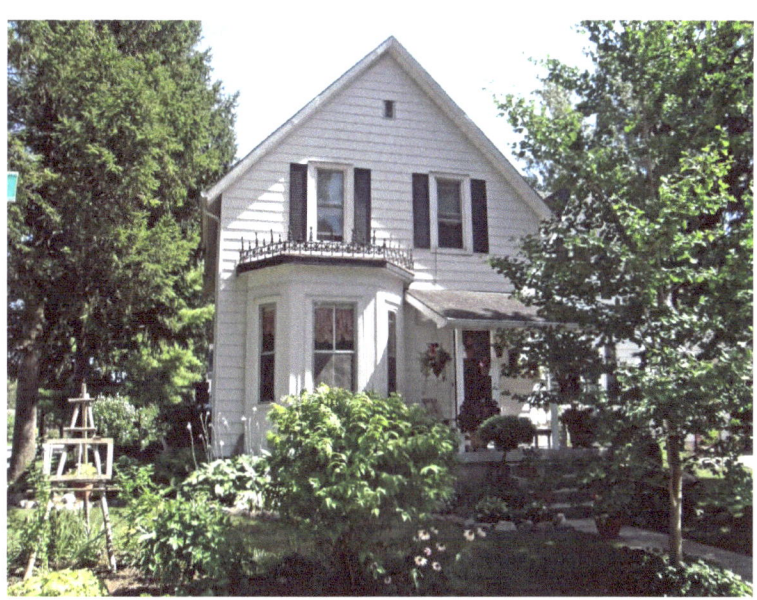

Wilson Street – Gothic Revival,
iron cresting above bay window

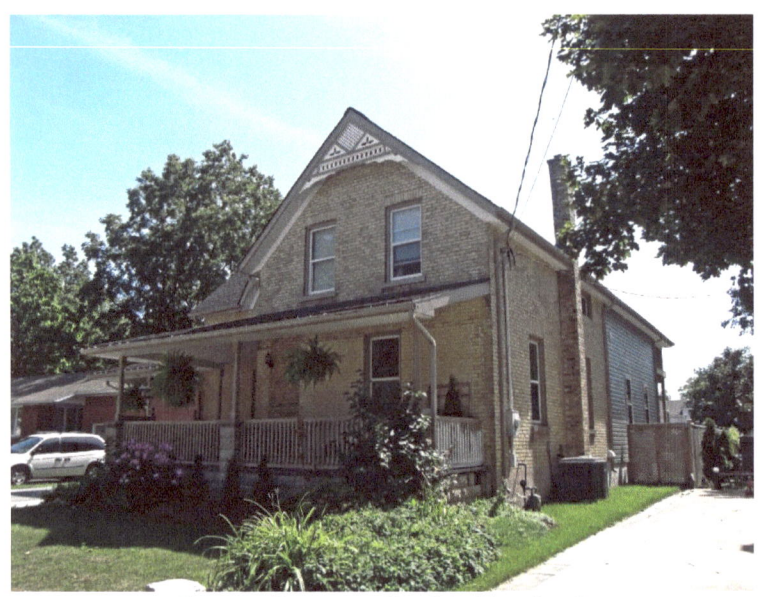

James Street – Gothic Revival

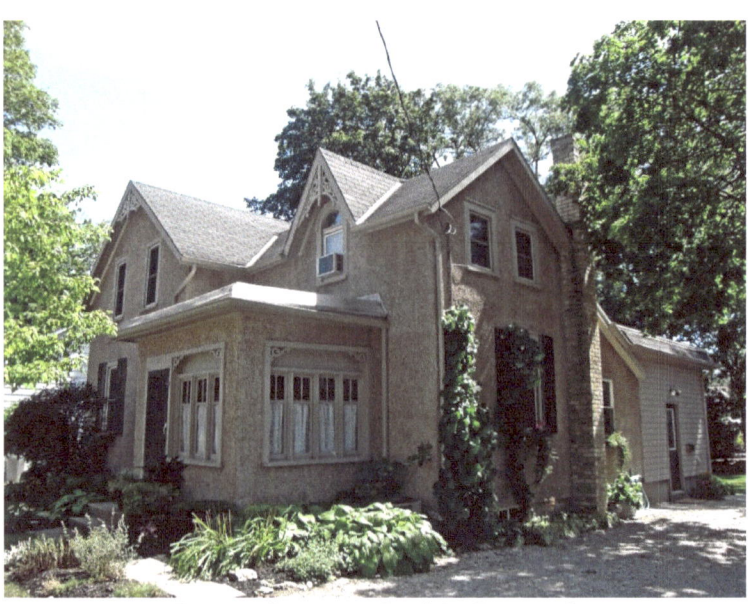

James Street – Gothic Revival

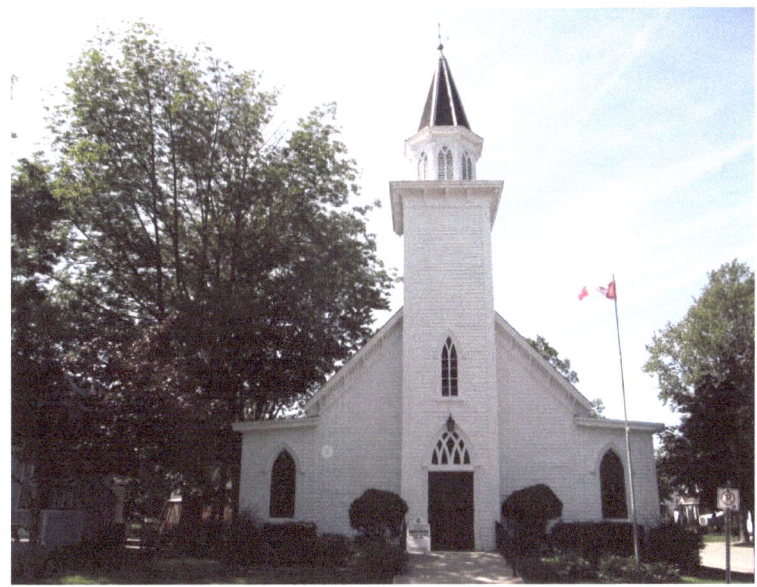

Jarvis Street – Church of England

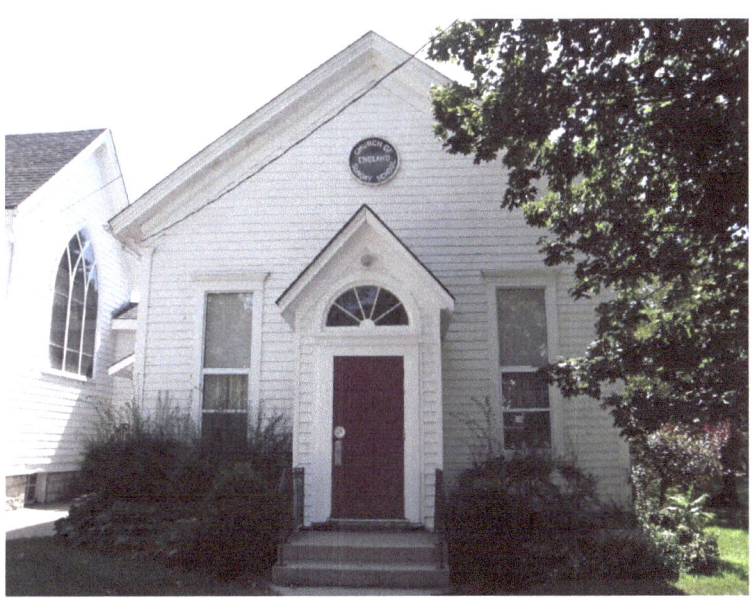

Church of England Sunday School

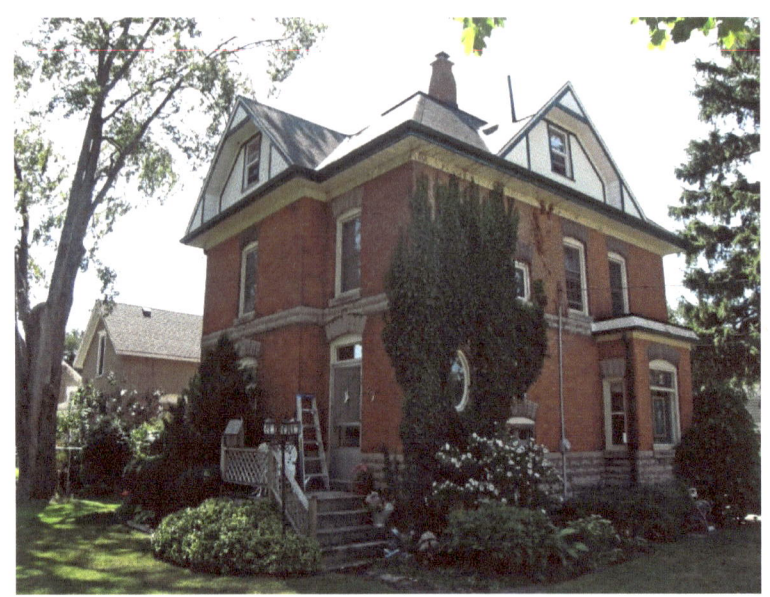

47 Jarvis Street

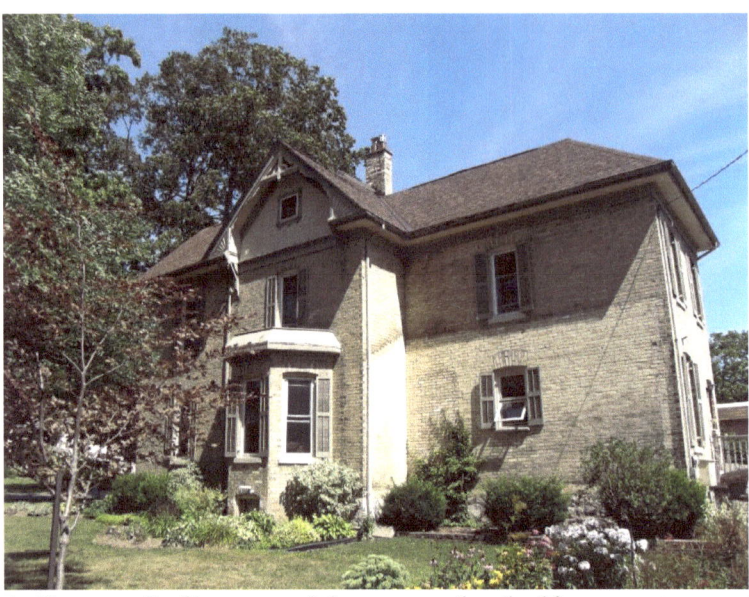

Jarvis Street – Italianate with two-and-a-half storey tower-like frontispiece with one-storey bay window

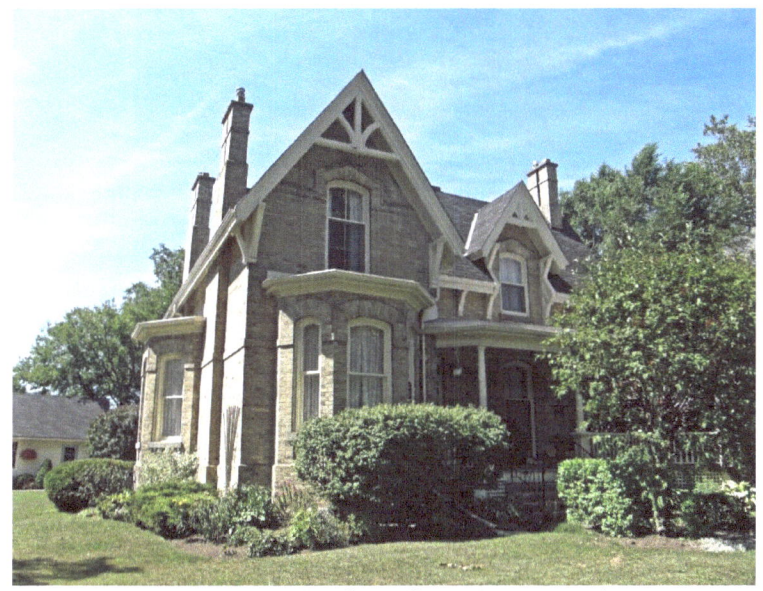

Gothic Revival – first floor bay windows

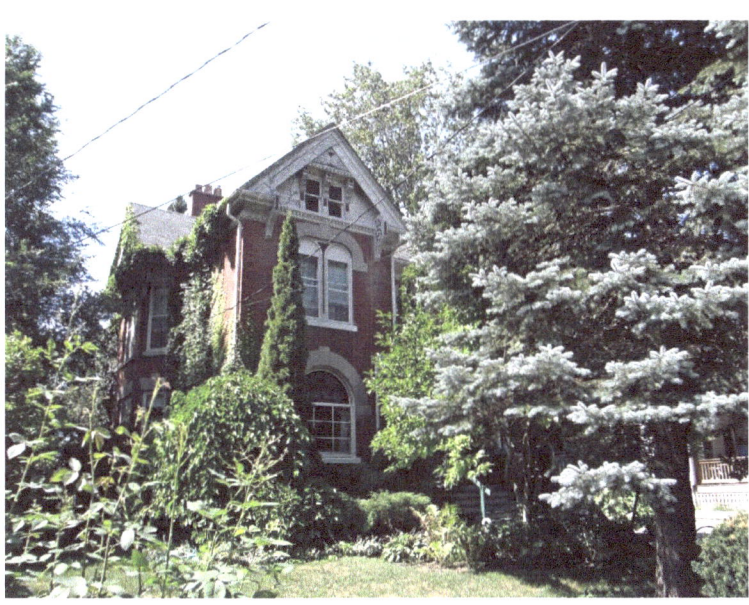

Romanesque style

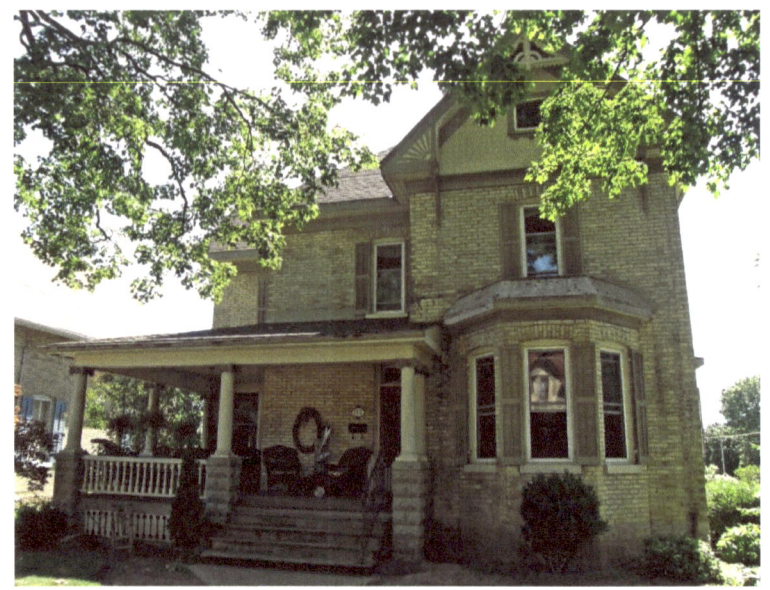

#115 - Italianate with two-and-a-half storey tower-like bay
– ionic capital on verandah pillars

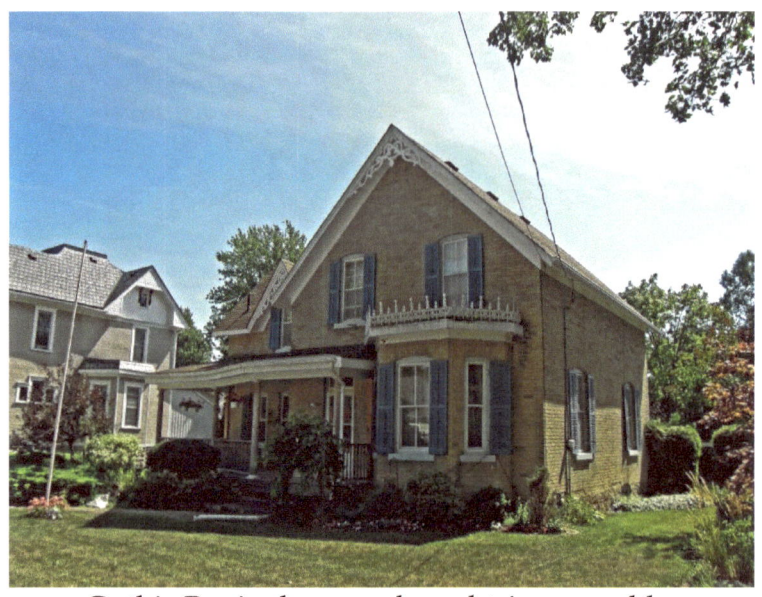

Gothic Revival – vergeboard trim on gable,
iron cresting above bay window

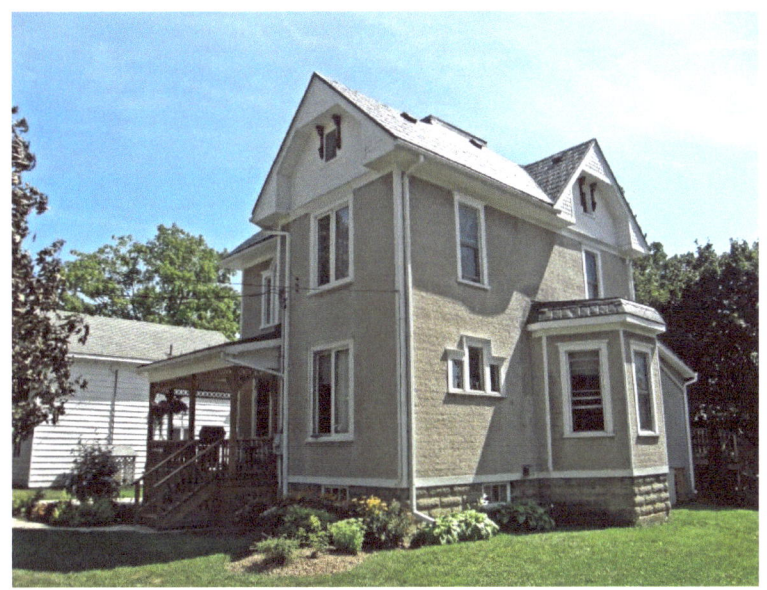

Edwardian style

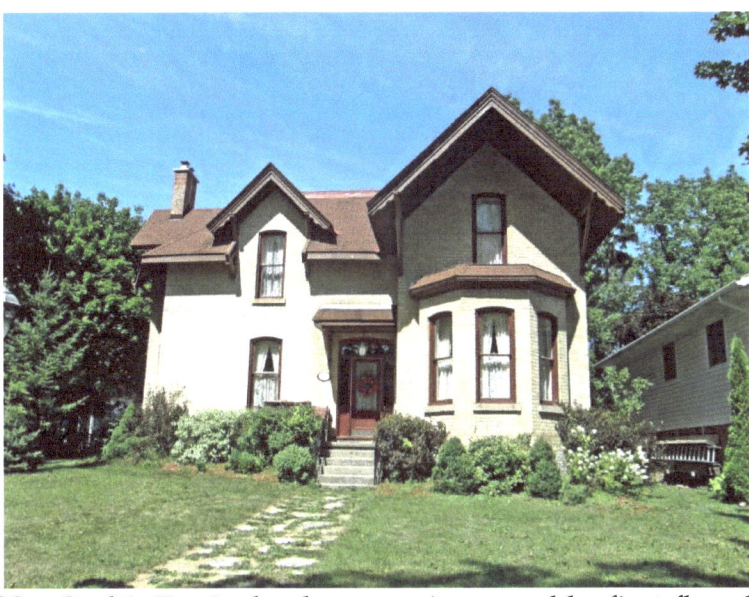

#120 – Gothic Revival – deep cornice on gable, first-floor bay window

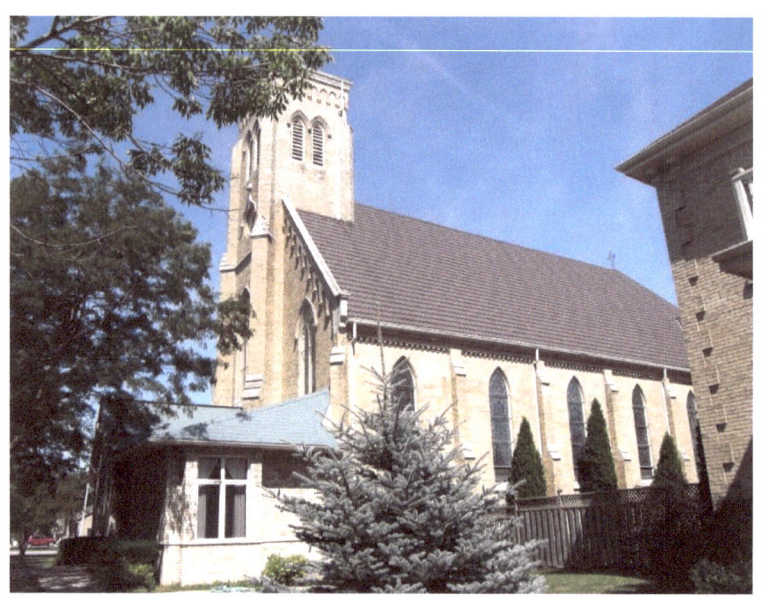

St. James Catholic Church – lancet windows

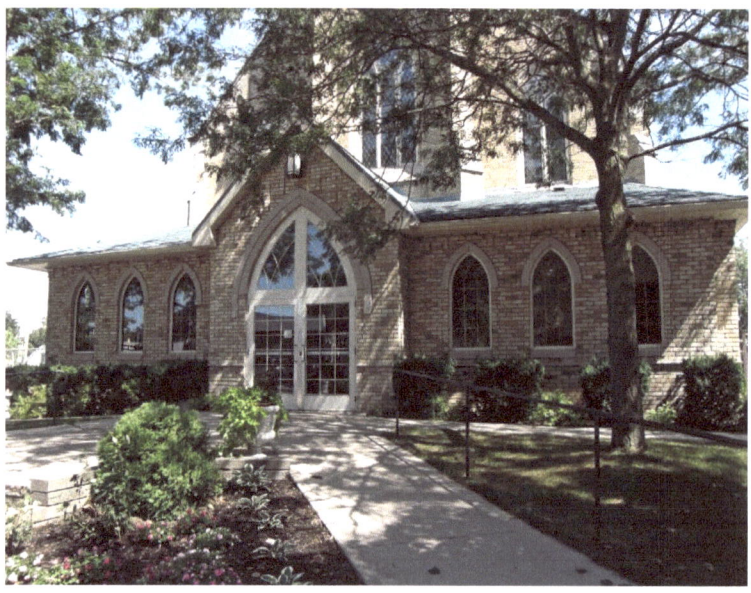

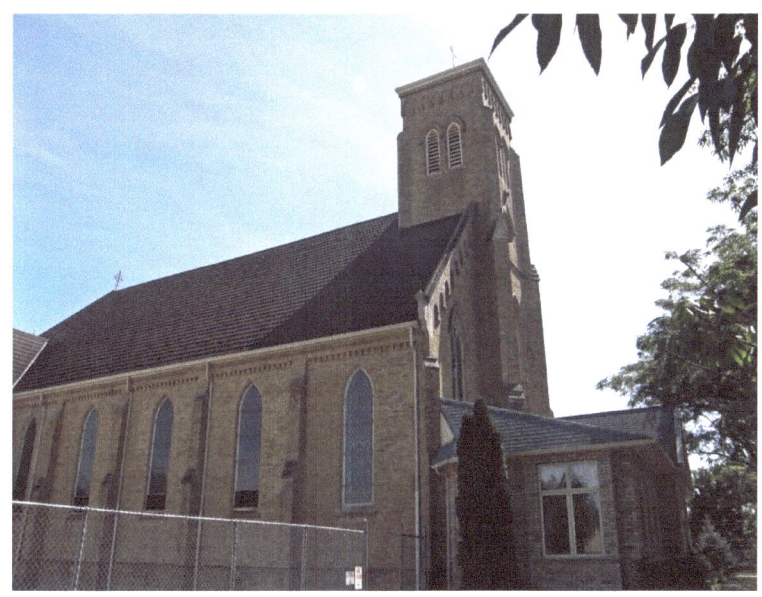

St. James Catholic Church

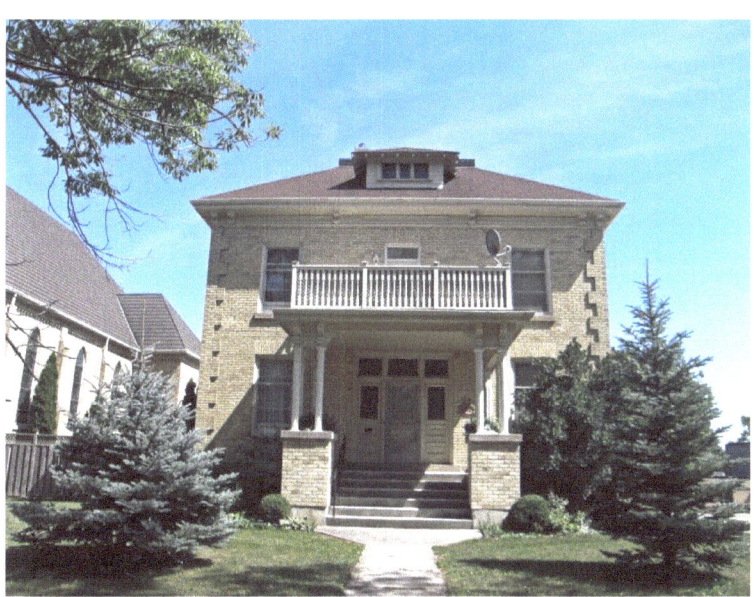

Italianate – dormer in attic, balcony on second floor

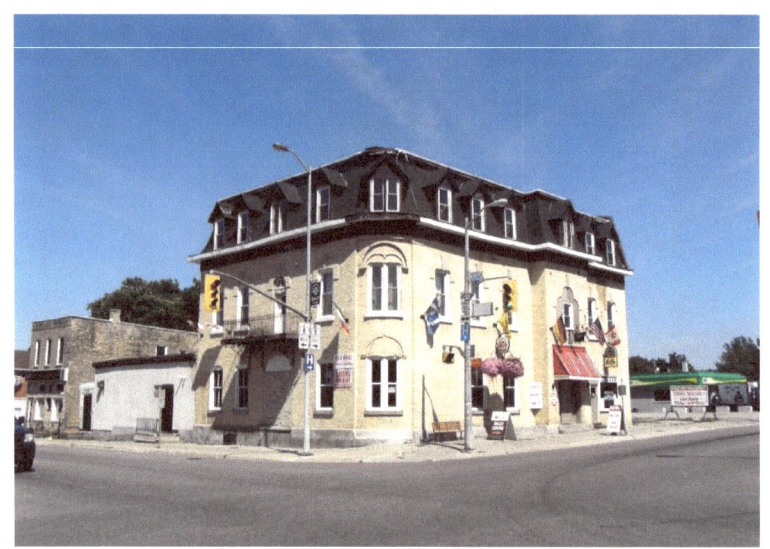

Second Empire – mansard roof with dormers

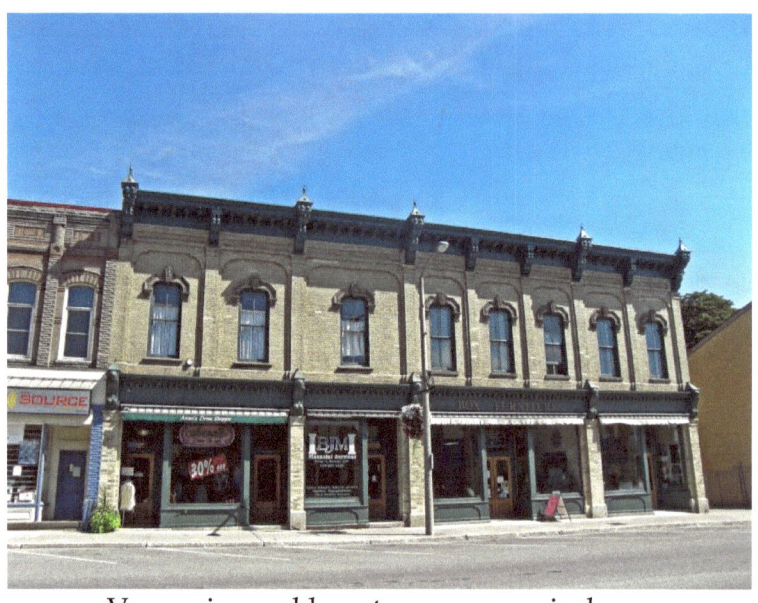

Voussoirs and keystones over windows

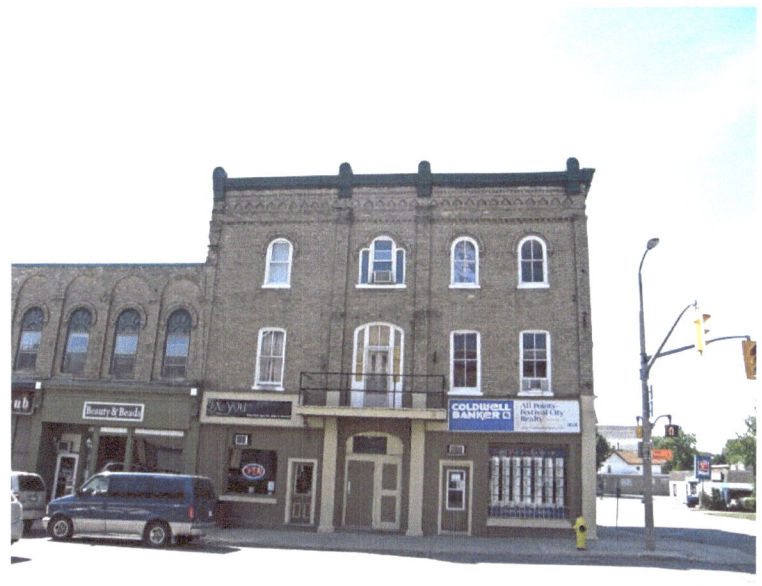

Arched window voussoirs, dentil moulding,
decorative brickwork, pilasters

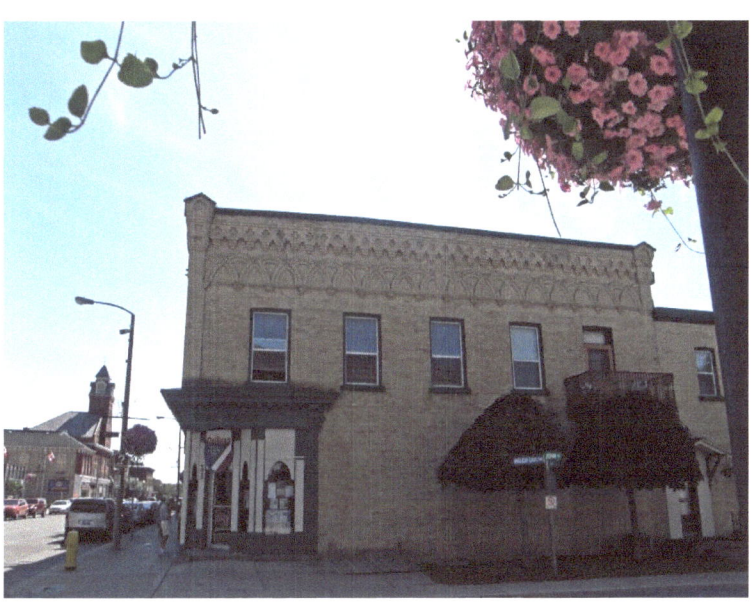

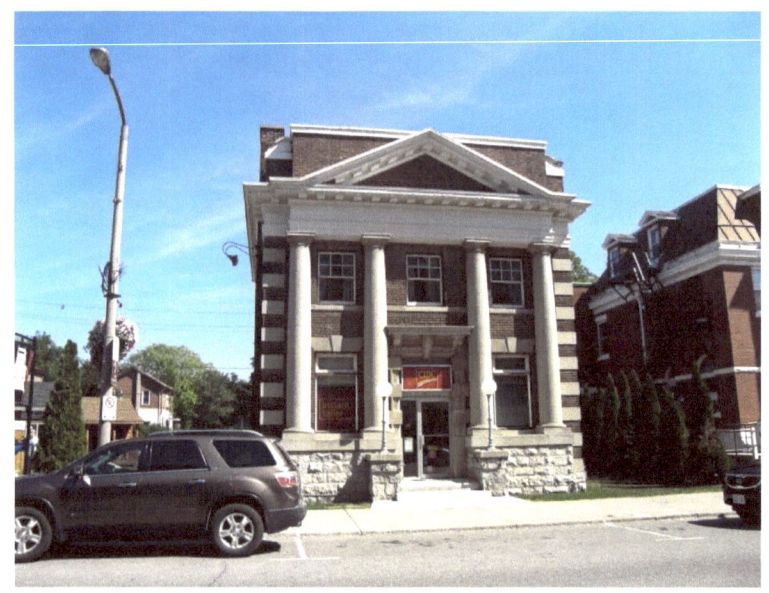

C.I.B.C. Bank – Beaux Arts style, corner quoins, pediment

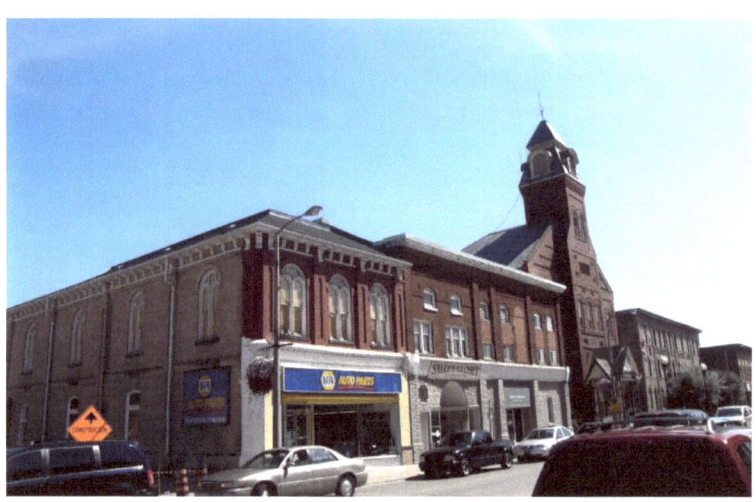

Downtown

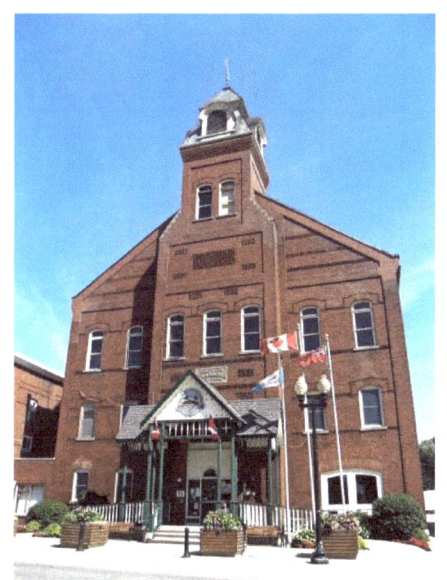

Seaforth Town Building A.D. 1893

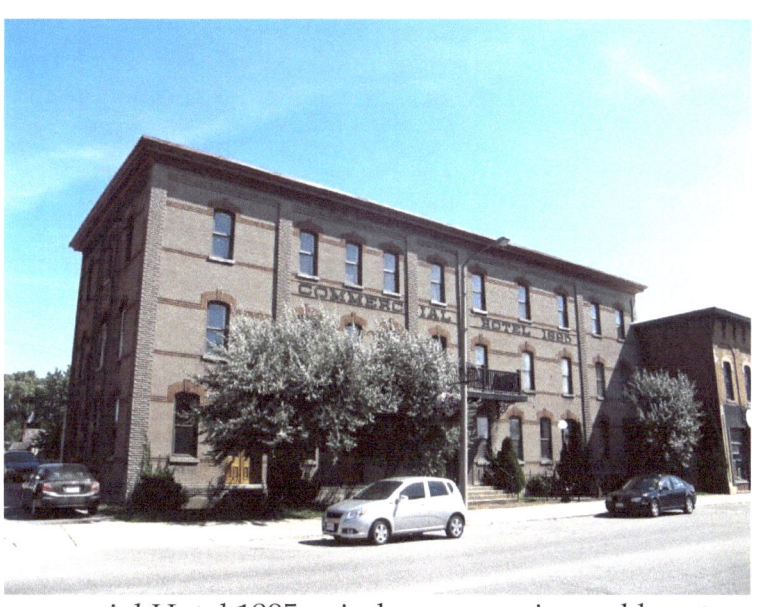

Commercial Hotel 1895, window voussoirs and keystones, dichromatic brickwork

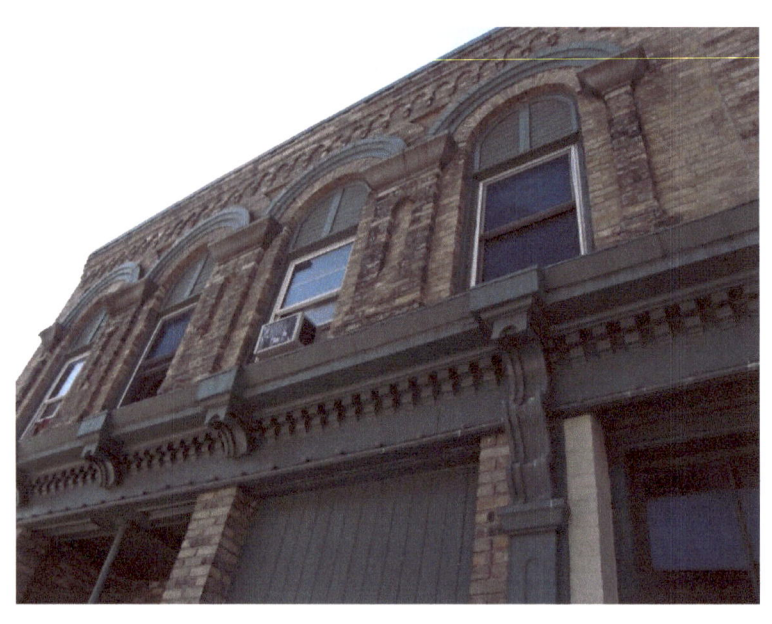

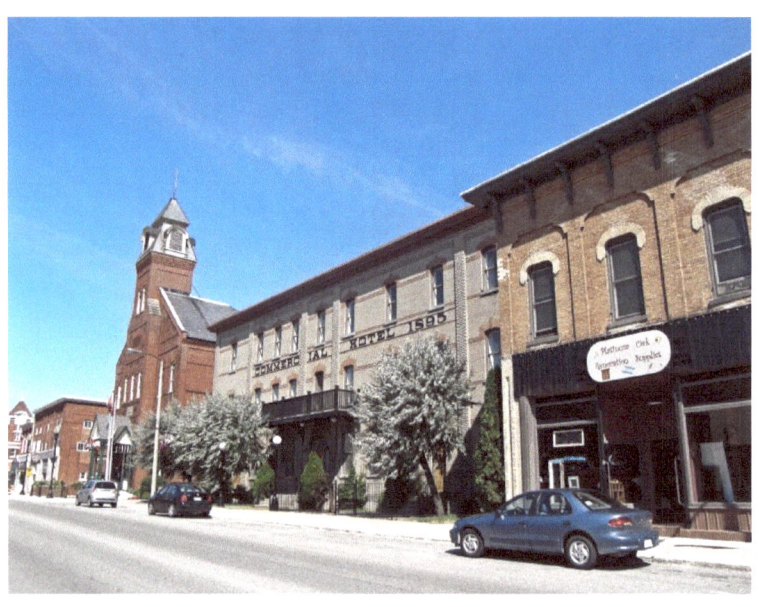

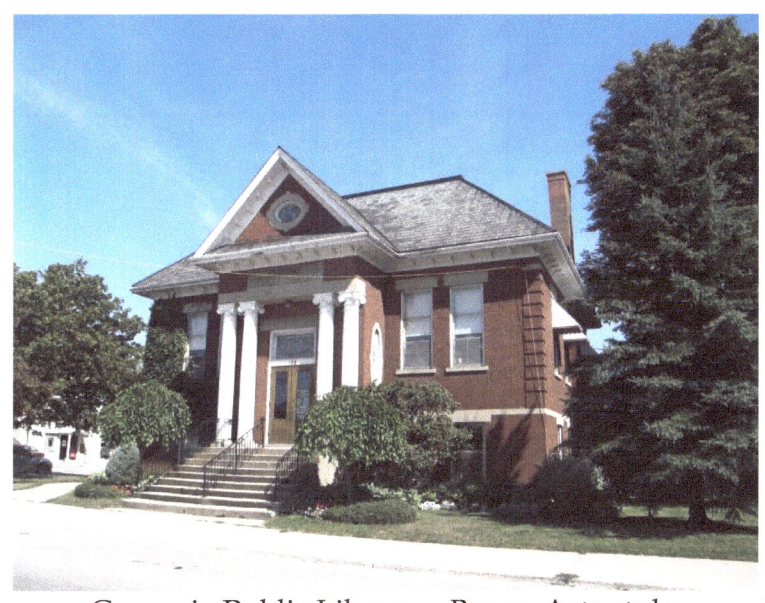

Carnegie Public Library – Beaux Arts style,
Ionic capitals on pillars, corner quoins

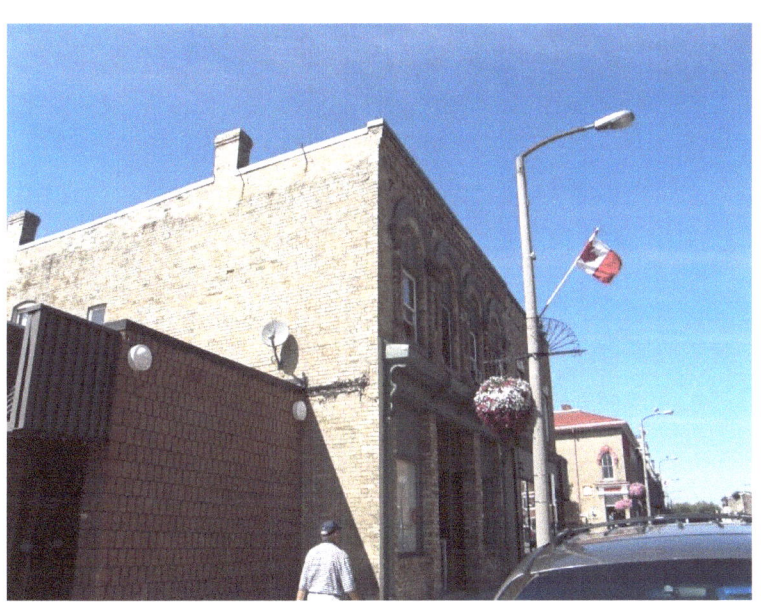

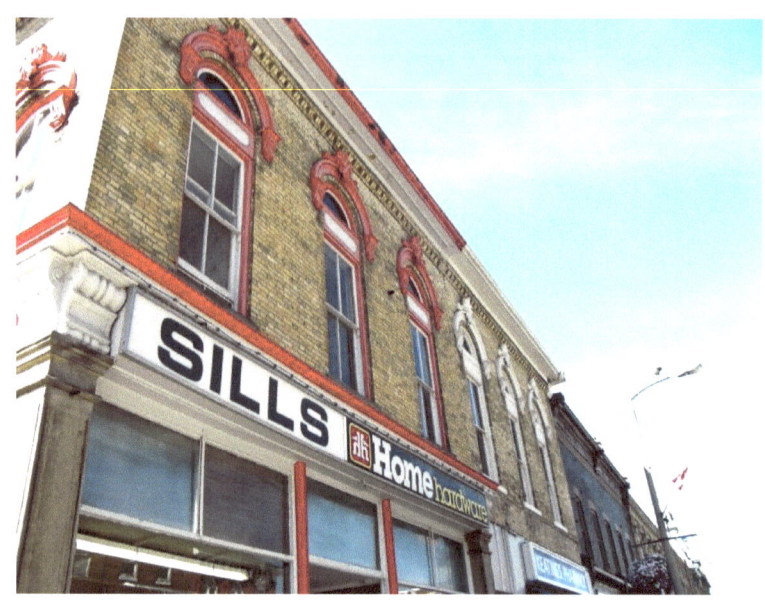

Colourful window arches, dentil moulding

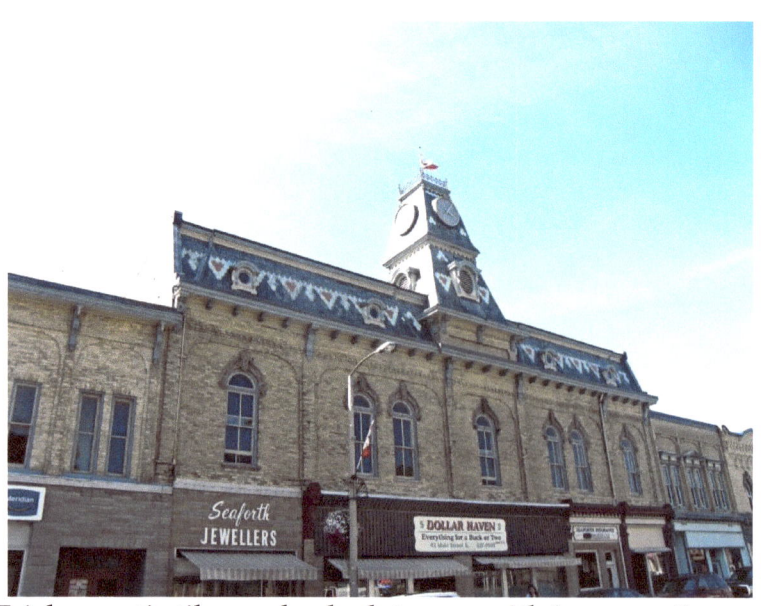

Trichromatic tile work, clock tower with iron cresting on rooftop, decorative voussoirs and keystones, dentil moulding, pilasters

Plowing Matches mural

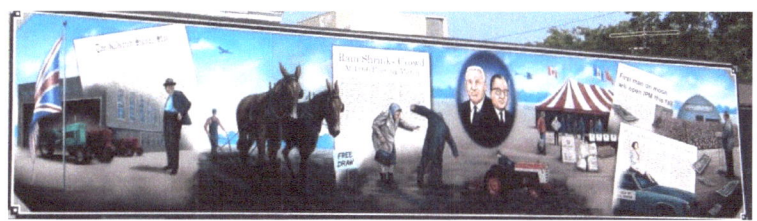

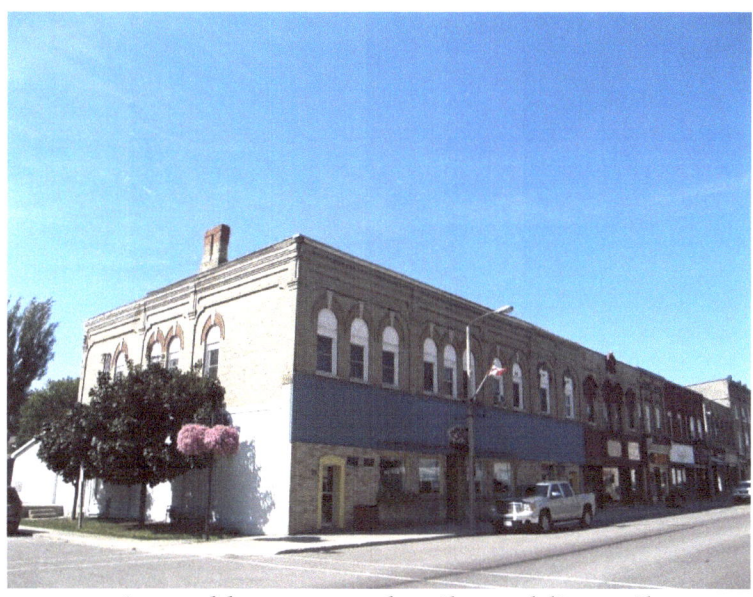

voussoirs and keystones, dentil moulding, pilasters

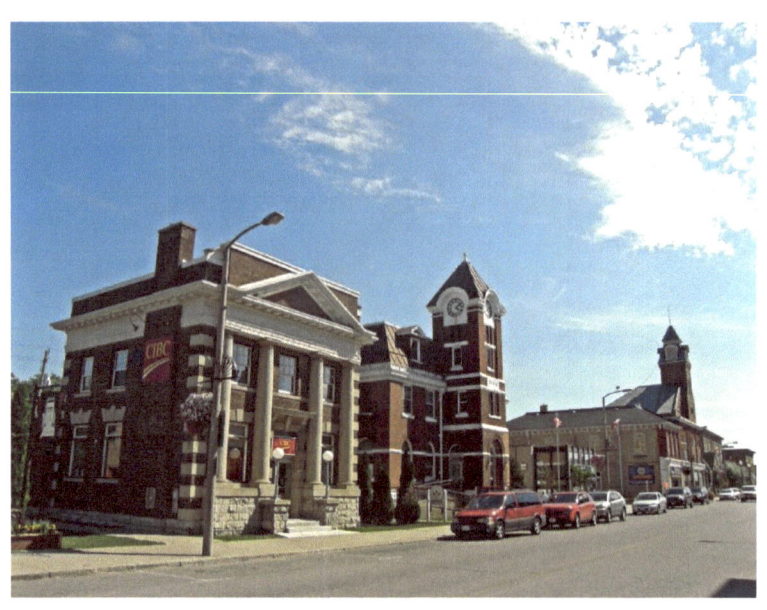

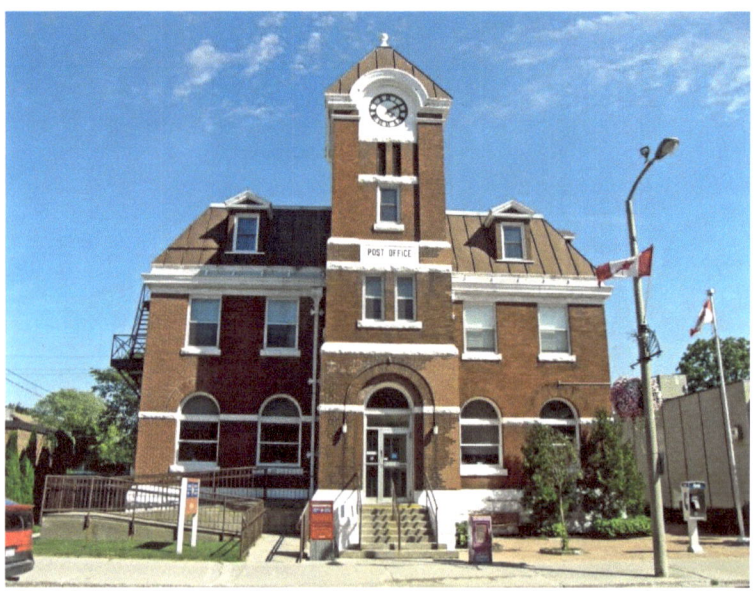

Post Office – centre clock tower, dormers in rooftop,
Romanesque style window and door voussoirs

Architectural Terms

Brackets: a decorative or weight-bearing structural element which forms a right angle with one side against a wall and the other under a projecting surface such as an eave or roof.	
Buttress: a masonry structure built against or projecting from a wall which serves to support or reinforce the wall. In Canadian architecture, they are sometimes used for decoration. Example: First Presbyterian Church	
Capitals (Ionic): The uppermost finish or decoration on a column. Example: Carnegie Public Library	
Cornice: originally the wooden overhang of the roof. With the use of stone, brick, iron and steel, the cornice is any projecting shelf at the top of a ceiling or roof. They can be very decorative. Example: #120	
Cornice Return: decorative element on the end of a gable. Example: Seaforth Manor, Helen Street	
Dentil Moulding: an even series of rectangles used as ornamental decoration in cornices.	

Dichromatic brickwork: the use of two colours of brick, tile or slate to decorate a façade. Trichromatic is the use of three colours. Example: downtown building with clock tower	
Dormer: (French for "sleep") a gable end window that pierces through the plane of a sloping roof surface to create usable space in the top floor or attic of a building by adding headroom.	
Frontispiece: a portion of the façade of a building, usually a centred doorway that is slightly raised from the rest of the building, usually has extensive ornamentation. Frontispieces are usually Classical in design with white columned porches.	
Gable: the triangular portion of a wall between the edges of a sloping roof.	
Hipped Roof: a roof where all sides slope downwards to the walls with no gables.	
Iron Cresting: A decorative ornament along the top of a roof. Iron cresting was popular in the Baroque era and also in Italianate, Victorian, Second Empire and Queen Anne styles of architecture. Example: #119	

Lancet Window: a tall, narrow window with a pointed arch at its top. Example: First Presbyterian Church	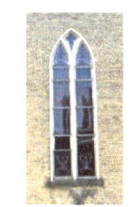
Pediment: a triangular section above the horizontal structure (entablature), typically supported by columns. The inside of the triangle is called the tympanum. Example: CIBC Bank Building	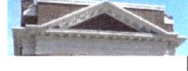
Pilaster: a slightly projecting column built into or applied to the face of a wall for additional structural support. Example: Downtown building	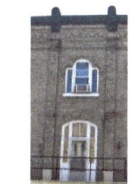
Quoin: masonry blocks at the corner of a wall, often a decorative feature, usually larger or of a different colour than the rest of the wall. Example: Carnegie Public Library	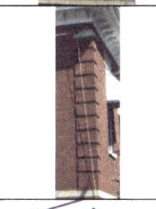
Vergeboards: also called bargeboards – hang from the projecting end of a roof and are often elaborately carved and ornamented. Example: #17	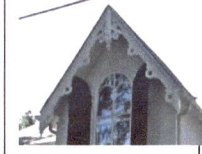
Voussoirs and Keystones a voussoir is a wedge-shaped element used in building an arch. A keystone is the central stone that locks all the stones into position, allowing the arch to bear weight. A keystone is often enlarged and embellished.	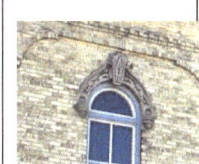

Seaforth Building Styles

Beaux Arts: Promoters of this style sought to express the classical principles on a grand and imposing scale. Many of the Beaux Arts buildings were banks, post offices, and railway stations. The Ontario Beaux Arts style is eclectic mixing elements of Classical, Renaissance and Baroque. Often the designs have a temple-like façade, pedimented porticos, balustrades, capitals in many styles Example: Seaforth Public Library	
Edwardian, 1900-1930 – This style bridges the ornate and elaborate styles of the Victorian era and the simplified styles of the 20th century. Balanced facades, simple roof lines, dormer windows, large front porches, and smooth brick surfaces are its characteristics. Example:	
Gothic Revival, 1830-1890 – These decorative buildings have sharply-pitched gables with highly detailed vergeboards, pointed-arch window openings, and dichromatic brickwork. It is a common style in Ontario.	
Italianate, 1850-1900 – It has wide-bracketed eaves, belvederes, wrap-around verandahs.	

Queen Anne, 1885-1900 – This style is distinguished by an irregular outline featuring a combination of an offset tower, broad gables, projecting two-storey bays, verandahs, multi-sloped roofs, and tall, decorative chimneys. A mixture of brick and wood is common. Windows often have one large single-paned bottom sash and small panes in the upper sash.	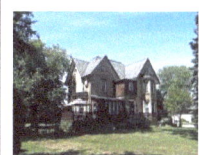
Romanesque Revival, 1880-1910 – This style hearkens back to medieval architecture of the 11th and 12th centuries with a heavy appearance, blocky towers and rounded arches.	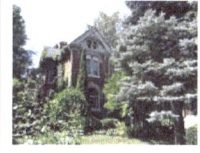

www.ingramcontent.com/pod-product-compliance
Lightning Source LLC
Chambersburg PA
CBHW041142180526

45159CB00002BB/705

9 781500 473730